DISCARD

CORNERSTONES OF FREEDOM™

The PERSIAN GULF WAR

BY JOSH GREGORY

CHILDREN'S PRESS®
An Imprint of Scholastic Inc.
New York Toronto London Auckland Sydney
Mexico City New Delhi Hong Kong
Danbury, Connecticut

BRINGING HISTORY to LIFE

Content Consultant
Christopher Gelpi, PhD
Professor of Political Science
Duke University
Charlotte, North Carolina

Library of Congress Cataloging-in-Publication Data

Gregory, Josh.
The Persian Gulf War/by Josh Gregory.
p. cm.—(Cornerstones of freedom)
Includes bibliographical references and index.
ISBN-13: 978-0-531-25038-9 (lib. bdg.) ISBN-10: 0-531-25038-5 (lib. bdg.)
ISBN-13: 978-0-531-26563-5 (pbk.) ISBN-10: 0-531-26563-3 (pbk.)
1. Persian Gulf War, 1991—Juvenile literature. I. Title.
DS79.723.G74 2012
956.7044'2—dc22 2011009491

Printed in the United States of America 113

1 2 3 4 5 6 7 8 9 10 R 21 20 19 18 17 16 15 14 13 12

Photographs © 2012: AP Images: 14, 49 (Nabil al-Jourani), back cover, 18, 52 (Bob Daugherty), 22 (Ron Edmonds), 4 bottom, 30 (Dieter Endlicher), 35 (Michel Euler), 45 (Greg Gibson), 28 (Pierre Gleizes), 48 (Bill Haber), 40 (Gene Herrick), 46 (INA), 4 top, 20 (Hasan Jamali), 54 (Liya Kochavi), 47 (Stephanie McGehee), 42 (Laurent Rebours), 55 (Bob Strong), 50, 51 (UNSCOM), 5 bottom, 8, 24, 57; Corbis Images: 15 (Patrick Durand/Sygma), 58 (INA), 21 (Rick Maiman/Sygma), 7, 12 (Jacques Pavlovsky/Sygma), 23 (Ron Sachs/CNP/Sygma), 10 (Shepard Sherbell/CORBIS SABA), 26, 44 (Peter Turnley); Getty Images: 25 (AFP), 6 (Francoise De Mulder/Roger Viollet), cover (Pascal Guyot/AFP), 41 (Bob Pearson/AFP), 34 (Diana Walker/Time Life Pictures); Josh Gregory: 64; ShutterStock, Inc./Nasser Buhamad: 17, 53; U.S. Army Photo: 33 (Sgt. Brian Cumper), 29 (Spc. David Faas), 36, 59 (JO1 Joe Gawlowicz), 37 (JOC Gloria Montgomery), 27, 56 (Russell Roederer), 2, 3, 38; Vector-Images.com: 5 top, 13.

Did you know that studying history can be fun?

BRING HISTORY TO LIFE by becoming a history investigator. Examine the evidence (primary and secondary source materials); cross-examine the people and witnesses. Take a look at what was happening at the time—but be careful! What happened years ago might suddenly become incredibly interesting and change the way you think!

Contents

SETTING THE SCENE

Oil and Politics

Crude oil is refined into a number of petroleum products that are essential in modern life.

Oil is one of the most important resources on Earth. We need it to power our vehicles and manufacture the thousands of different products we use every day. More than half of the world's oil reserves are located in the

THE PERSIAN GULF WAR IS ALSO

Middle East. Most of this oil is in Saudi Arabia, Iran, Iraq, and Kuwait. This region has become increasingly important to the rest of the world as oil consumption has increased over time. Powerful nations such as the United States, Great Britain, and Russia keep a close watch on political developments in the Middle East.

Many Middle Eastern countries have a long history of fighting among themselves. The conflicts stem from social, historical, political, and religious differences. Most Middle Eastern people are Muslim. But there are several different sects, or groups, within the religion. They share fundamental Islamic beliefs. But their divisions have often led to violence and impacted the rest of the world.

Iraq is one of the world's biggest oil producers.

CHAPTER 1

THE INVASION OF KUWAIT

Saddam Hussein came to power in 1979.

On July 16, 1979, Saddam Hussein became president of the Middle Eastern country of Iraq. Saddam had been a member of the Ba'ath political party since 1957. In 1968, the Ba'ath Party took control of Iraq. Saddam became one of the most powerful men in the country. When President Ahmad Hasan al-Bakr resigned in 1979, Saddam took office.

Saddam swiftly began to exercise powerful influence over government affairs. He brutally attacked his political opponents. People who questioned his authority often were found dead or went missing. He used an extensive network of spies to prevent any potential **resistance** to his rule.

Saddam Hussein had his image put on billboards and statues throughout Iraq.

Most of the people in Iraq follow the Shiite sect of Islam. But Saddam was a Sunni Muslim. He was known for his cruelty toward those people who did not share his religious beliefs.

Building a Military

In September 1980, the Iraqi military invaded the neighboring country of Iran. They hoped to gain control of the territory called Shatt al Arab. The territory is valuable because of its rights to certain bodies of water and access to the Persian Gulf. The two countries fought for eight years in what became known as the Iran-Iraq War before agreeing to a cease-fire initiated by the **United Nations**. Hundreds of thousands of Iraqi and Iranian troops were killed.

Saddam spent a great deal of money to build up Iraq's military during the war. Iraq had the fourth-largest military in the world when the war ended. Saddam had more than one million soldiers and 5,700 tanks at his disposal. The Iraqi military was well trained and ready for battle.

Iraq's scientists were developing **weapons of mass destruction** at this time. They created chemical weapons such as **nerve gas** and special **artillery** shells to launch

A VIEW FROM ABROAD

Although Saddam was a cruel leader, he sometimes used his power for Iraq's benefit. In 1972, he helped nationalize Iraq's oil industry. This allowed the government to make a great deal of money from the country's oil production. After becoming president, Saddam used oil money to improve Iraq. He funded new medical facilities, improved the educational system, and built new roads.

Iraq purchased many new weapons during the Iran-Iraq War.

the gas at their enemies. They worked on biological weapons, which can cause diseases and destroy crops. Scientists also began to make progress toward arming Iraq with nuclear weapons.

In order to pay for his new military and weapons, Saddam drove Iraq deep into debt. He borrowed huge amounts of money from neighboring countries such as Kuwait. Iraq owed its neighbors about $80 billion by the end of the Iran-Iraq War. Even with the money the oil industry brought in, Saddam could not pay back such huge sums. The U.S. government believed that this massive debt would encourage Saddam to be peaceful and cooperative. This behavior would bring stability to the Middle East. But the United States underestimated Saddam's hunger for power.

SPOTLIGHT ON

OPEC

OPEC has often had a major effect on the world economy since its formation in 1960. The organization sets limits on how much oil each country can produce. It also sets a minimum price for oil to prevent countries from getting into price wars. In 1973, the organization called for a 70 percent price increase. These increases continued throughout the decade. Prices eventually reached 10 times what they had been in 1973. This caused oil shortages in many Western countries and contributed to worldwide **inflation**. By 1975, there were 13 member nations in OPEC. Today, there are 12.

Economic Warfare

In 1960, several Middle Eastern countries and the South American country of Venezuela joined together to form the Organization of the **Petroleum** Exporting Countries (OPEC). OPEC was designed to help its member countries make as much money as they could from the sale of oil by not competing with one another.

In 1990, the country of Kuwait began producing more oil than the OPEC **quota** allowed. Kuwait is a member of OPEC. It is located along Iraq's southeastern border. Kuwait was also selling its oil at lower prices.

With so much oil available at low prices, demand for Iraq's oil decreased.

Saddam believed that Kuwait was stealing oil from Iraq by drilling into the Rumaila oil field in an area past the countries' shared border. He claimed that the people of Kuwait had become wealthy by taking oil that rightfully belonged to Iraq. He also accused the Kuwaiti people of showing off this wealth by living lives of luxury. "War doesn't mean just tanks, artillery, or ships," said Saddam. He called Kuwait's actions economic warfare.

The Rumaila oil field lies near the Iraq-Kuwait border.

Sheikh Jaber Al-Ahmed Al-Sabah led Kuwait from 1977 until his death in 2006.

Growing Tensions

The cost of maintaining his large army prompted Saddam to launch a plan to get out of debt. He claimed that Iraq had saved the rest of the Middle East from Iranian expansion by fighting in the Iran-Iraq War. He demanded that Kuwait forgive Iraq's debt as repayment for this service. Kuwait refused.

A FIRSTHAND LOOK AT
A PEACEFUL SOLUTION

In July 1990, American diplomat April Glaspie met with Saddam to discuss tensions between Kuwait and Iraq. Saddam claimed that he was willing to reach a peaceful solution to the issue. Glaspie's report to officials in Washington, D.C., indicated that the conflict would likely be solved with negotiations. It also stated that Saddam was interested in friendship with the United States. See page 60 for a link to view the document.

Saddam realized that he would be unable to maintain a large military if Iraq continued to carry the debt. But he would not decrease the size of the military. He decided to invade Kuwait and claim it as part of Iraq. Such an invasion would cancel his debt, increase Iraq's oil reserves, and expand his power in the Middle East.

To justify his plans, Saddam claimed that Kuwait had once been part of the southern Iraqi province of Basra. He reasoned that it made perfect sense for the two nations to be joined once again. But his claims were not true.

The Invasion

Iraqi forces began to build up along the Iraq-Kuwait border in July 1990. Kuwait is a small country. It had a population of 1.9 million people at the time. Its military was tiny and weak compared to the massive and experienced Iraqi forces.

The Iraqi Republican Guard invaded Kuwait on August 2, at 1:00 a.m. The Republican Guard was a special branch of the military that took orders directly from Saddam. Fifty thousand of Iraq's most highly trained troops went up against the 16,000-man Kuwaiti army. The Republican Guard quickly made its way into the country. They reached the capital, Kuwait City, by about 5:30 a.m. Sheikh Jaber, the Kuwaiti leader, had already fled to the neighboring country of Saudi Arabia with his family. The Kuwaiti forces in Kuwait City surrendered. Kuwait now belonged to Saddam.

The Republican Guard almost immediately headed south to the border that Kuwait shared with Saudi Arabia. Troops were planted on either side of the highway connecting the two nations. The world waited for Saddam's next move.

Kuwait City is a Western-style, modern city of 2.38 million people.

CHAPTER 2

OPERATION DESERT SHIELD

King Fahd (left) hoped President George H. W. Bush would help defend Saudi Arabia from Iraq.

KING FAHD OF SAUDI ARABIA spoke on the phone with U.S. president George H. W. Bush as the Iraqi troops gathered near the border. King Fahd had already spoken to Saddam. Saddam informed the king that Iraq was now in control of Kuwait and would never allow the Kuwaiti royal family to return. King Fahd asked Saddam to consider leaving Kuwait. He also made it clear that Saudi Arabia would not recognize Saddam as the ruler of Kuwait. "I believe nothing will work with Saddam but the use of force," King Fahd confided to President Bush.

Like many Middle Eastern countries, Saudi Arabia has a very large supply of oil.

The Importance of Saudi Arabia

Saudi Arabia was the Middle East's largest oil producer. Iraq was already in control of about 20 percent of the world's total oil reserves. Taking Saudi Arabia would push that total above 50 percent. Many people feared that this could cause an oil crisis around the world.

Saudi Arabia's military consisted of 70,000 troops. Saddam's forces would easily overpower them. Once they did, they would also have control of Saudi Arabia's ports along the Persian Gulf. If the United States were to become involved, U.S. forces would have to land on Saudi Arabia's west coast. Then they would have to trek across 500 miles (805 kilometers) of desert to reach the Iraqis.

The United Nations Takes a Stand

The United States and Kuwait requested a meeting of the United Nations (UN) Security Council in New York City on August 2. Representatives from world powers such as China, France, Great Britain, and the Soviet Union met to discuss the situation in the Middle East. They quickly passed UN Resolution 660. The resolution demanded that Saddam remove his troops from Kuwait immediately.

Saddam did not comply. The UN passed Resolution 661 four days later. It called for a worldwide ban on trade with Iraq. This kept necessary supplies out of Iraq. It also prevented Iraq from selling oil to most of its biggest customers, who were all members of the United Nations. These threats did not persuade Saddam to withdraw from Kuwait.

The UN Security Council includes members from around the globe.

A FIRSTHAND LOOK AT

PRESIDENT GEORGE H. W. BUSH'S PRESS CONFERENCE

President Bush gave a press conference about the situation in Kuwait on August 5, 1990. It was here that he spoke the famous words, "This will not stand. This will not stand, this aggression against Kuwait." His statement signaled to the world that the United States was seriously considering getting involved in the conflict. See page 60 for a link to view President Bush's statement.

Decision Time

Eleven **divisions** of Iraqi troops had gathered near the Saudi border by August 6. They were there to threaten Saudi Arabia and to be prepared to fight back if the United States got involved. U.S. leaders quickly gathered to make a decision about the situation. They needed to send troops soon if they were going to get involved.

President Bush speaks to the press about Iraq's aggression against Kuwait.

Secretary of Defense Dick Cheney (left) worked to convince King Fahd to allow U.S. troops into Saudi Arabia.

U.S. general Colin Powell believed that the American people would not want to send their soldiers to die to protect the interests of wealthy Kuwaiti oil sheikhs. The American people were more likely to understand the danger the world faced if Saddam took control of Saudi Arabia. "I think we'd go to war over Saudi Arabia," Powell said to General Norman Schwarzkopf, "but I doubt we'd go to war over Kuwait."

General Schwarzkopf and Secretary of Defense Dick Cheney traveled to Saudi Arabia on August 7 to meet with King Fahd and his son, Prince Bandar. They presented their plan for driving the Iraqi forces out of

General Schwarzkopf (right) promised King Fahd that the United States would defend Saudi Arabia at any cost.

Kuwait. King Fahd was concerned that the Americans would not see the war through to its end. He feared this would leave Saudi Arabia undefended. Schwarzkopf and Cheney promised that the United States was willing to do everything in its power to defend Saudi Arabia from the Iraqis. They also promised to leave as soon as Iraq was driven from Kuwait.

Schwarzkopf showed King Fahd photographs of Iraqi tanks at the Saudi border. Some of the tanks were positioned on Saudi soil. The king agreed to allow the U.S. troops into Saudi Arabia. President Bush gave the order to begin sending troops to the region. The first U.S. troops began moving the next day as part of a UN

coalition. This buildup of troops would be known as Operation Desert Shield.

More Trouble in Kuwait

Life worsened for the people of Kuwait as other nations prepared for military action. Iraqi soldiers often treated them cruelly. Kuwaiti citizens lived in constant fear of arrest, torture, or even death.

Saddam even attacked the Kuwaitis' way of life. Phone lines were destroyed to prevent Kuwaitis from communicating with one another. Schools and businesses were shut down across the country. The Iraqis burned homes and bombed offices. Kuwaitis were forced to become Iraqi citizens in order to get supplies and food **rations**.

YESTERDAY'S HEADLINES

On August 23, 1990, Saddam appeared on Iraqi television with a group of Western hostages, mostly from Great Britain. They had been held by Iraq since its invasion of Kuwait. He told the nervous hostages that they were helping to achieve peace in the Middle East. People around the world thought the broadcast was designed to manipulate people into believing that Saddam was a friendly man who treated his hostages with kindness. The British foreign secretary called the broadcast "contemptible." A British newspaper reported the event with a headline that read "Outrage at Iraqi TV Hostage Show."

Some Kuwaitis fought back against the Iraqi invaders.

Iraqi forces surrounded foreign embassies. They starved out ambassadors and captured them. Saddam purposely moved many of his Western hostages to important factories and military locations. This was done to discourage coalition forces from attacking these places.

The Kuwaiti military had been shut down after its surrender. But some Kuwaiti civilians fought on. They formed resistance groups to spread anti-Iraq messages and carry out small attacks on Iraqi soldiers at night. Unfortunately, their small numbers kept them from having a major effect on the situation.

General Norman Schwarzkopf

H. Norman Schwarzkopf was born in Trenton, New Jersey, on August 22, 1934. He studied at the U.S. Military Academy and entered the U.S. Army upon graduating in 1956. He served in the Vietnam War and continued to rise in rank in the years following. By 1988, he had achieved the rank of four-star general. Schwarzkopf was responsible for directing and organizing the entire UN coalition force during the Persian Gulf War.

A War on the Horizon

Large numbers of UN coalition forces gathered in Saudi Arabia as the weeks passed. It became clear that even this show of force would not convince Saddam to leave Kuwait. The name of the UN military operation was changed from Desert Shield to Desert Sword on October 26. UN forces were ready to attack whenever they were needed.

The UN Security Council met on October 29 to pass Resolution 674. It officially allowed force to be

Hostages from France, Great Britain, the United States, and other countries were finally freed by Saddam in December 1990.

used on Iraq if it did not leave Kuwait. It also made Iraq financially responsible for the extensive damage it was causing to Kuwait.

Saddam allowed his many Western hostages to begin leaving Kuwait and Iraq on December 6. Countries around the world had been extremely critical of Iraq's treatment of these hostages. Saddam wanted to maintain what little goodwill he had left in the international community. The United Nations set a final deadline for Iraq 12 days later. Coalition forces would have full authorization to attack if the Iraqi forces did not begin withdrawing from Kuwait by January 15, 1991.

By the end of the year, Iraq had given no indication that it would follow the UN's orders. Meanwhile, the coalition forces had grown to more than 700,000 troops. Five hundred thousand were U.S. soldiers. The rest were provided by 33 other nations. Much of the world stood against Saddam. It looked as if there would be a war.

By the beginning of 1991, coalition forces were ready to attack Iraq.

CHAPTER 3

COMBAT IN THE DESERT

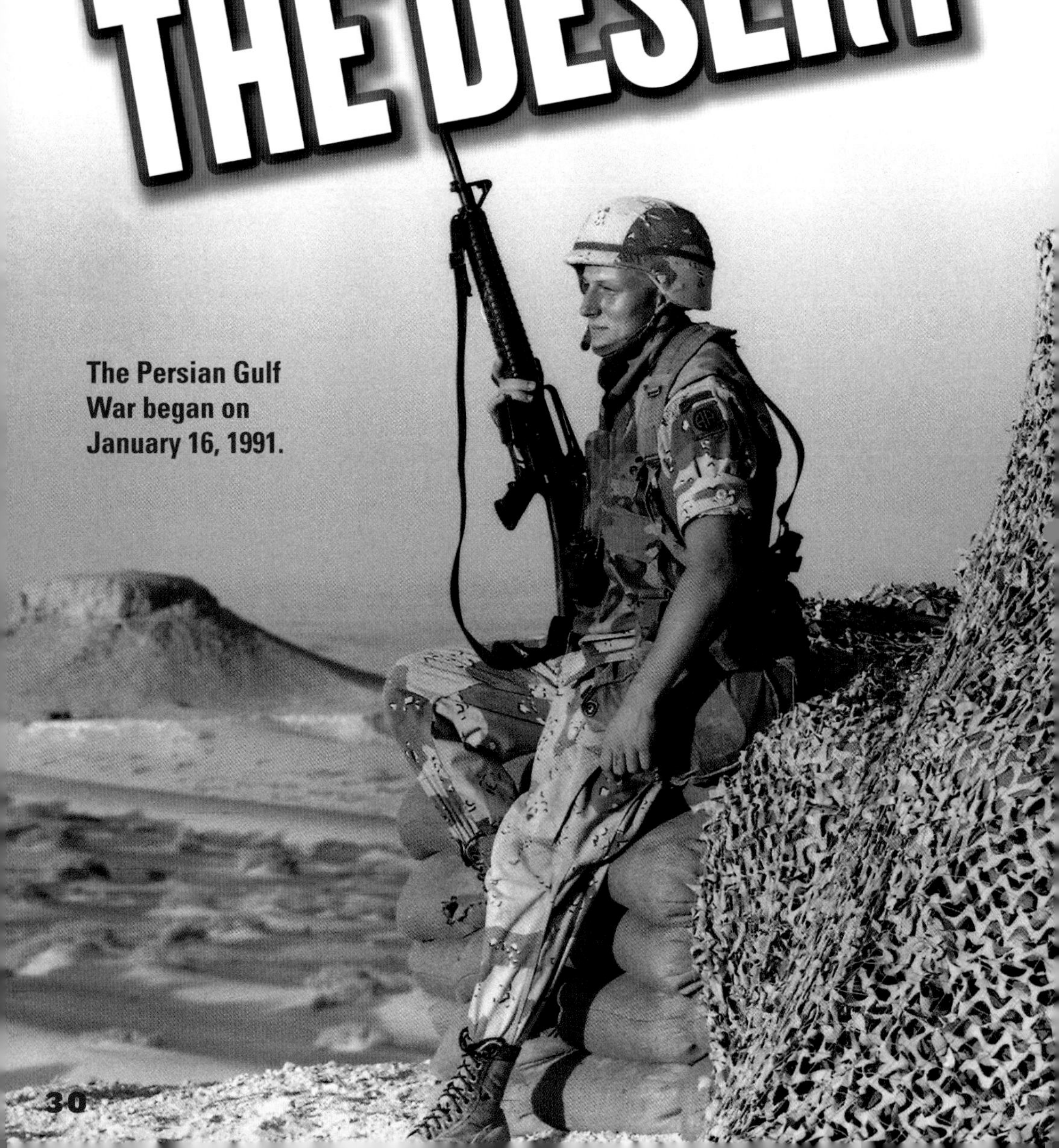

The Persian Gulf War began on January 16, 1991.

Even though the United Nations had voted to allow the use of force against the Iraqi troops in Kuwait, the U.S. government still had to decide whether its troops would be allowed to take part in combat. The U.S. Congress held a vote on January 12, 1991, to make the decision. Many in Congress did not want to go to war in the Middle East. The vote to fight barely passed. The UN deadline arrived three days later. The Iraqi troops had not moved from Kuwait.

A VIEW FROM ABROAD

Much of the world, including many Middle Eastern nations, stood against Saddam Hussein. But not everyone saw him as an enemy. Saddam often claimed that the Western world was attempting to corrupt Muslim beliefs and destroy the Middle Eastern way of life. Several other leaders agreed with him. Palestinian leader Yasser Arafat once referred to Saddam as an "Arab patriot." King Hussein of Jordan remained Saddam's ally during the Persian Gulf War. He believed that Saddam's actions in the Iran-Iraq War had saved the Arab world from Iran's Shiite influence.

The First Attacks

Fiery explosions lit up the night sky over Iraq in the early morning hours of January 16, 1991. The UN planes and helicopters had begun the assault. This phase of the Persian Gulf War was called Operation Desert Storm. The coalition's strategy was to conduct massive bombing raids to weaken the Iraqi forces before engaging in ground combat. Their first targets were Iraqi antiaircraft defenses. The raids destroyed most of these defenses very quickly. This allowed coalition planes to continue attacking by air with little fear of being shot down. Only three coalition aircraft were lost to Iraqi guns during the first 24 hours of the bombing.

UN helicopters attacked Iraq's radar systems. This left Iraqi forces with no way to detect incoming planes or

Helicopters helped cripple Iraqi communications.

missiles. Stealth jets flew to the Iraqi capital of Baghdad. They attacked Iraqi command centers with missiles. The destruction of these command centers made it difficult for Iraqi commanders to manage and communicate with troops in Kuwait.

Millions of people worldwide watched these events unfold on television. The Persian Gulf War was the first war to be broadcast live. Reporters in the Middle East could cover the events as they happened. They provided minute-by-minute updates to viewers around the world.

A FIRSTHAND LOOK AT

PRESIDENT BUSH'S ADDRESS TO THE NATION

President Bush addressed the United States in a national television appearance on January 16, 1991. He announced that air attacks had begun in Kuwait and Iraq. He also explained why these attacks were necessary. He said that all efforts to end the conflict peacefully had been tried and stated that the war's goal was simply to force the Iraqis out of Kuwait. See page 60 for a link to listen to the president's speech.

Attack on Israel

On January 18, Iraq began launching missiles at Israel, an ally of the United States. At least 17 people were injured over the next two days in the Israeli city of Tel Aviv. Israel immediately declared war against Iraq in **retaliation** for the attacks.

Bush's speech helped explain the United States' reasons for waging war on Iraq.

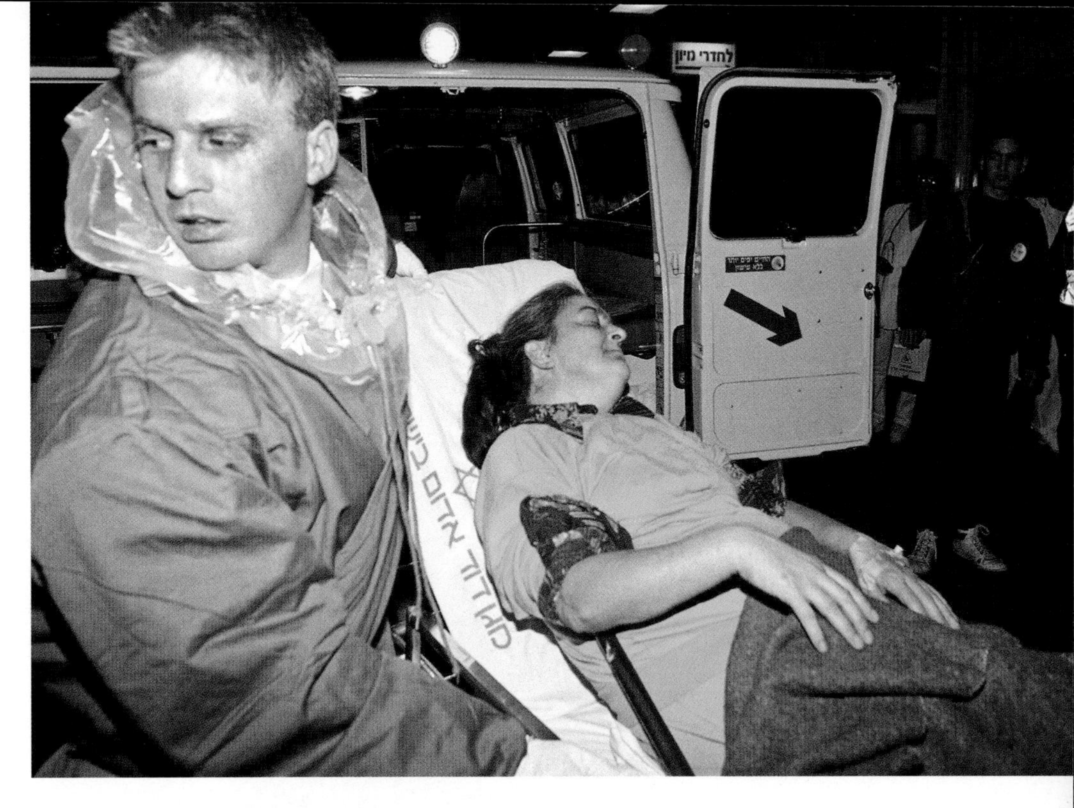

The attacks on Israel caused major destruction and injured and killed many innocent civilians.

The United States began negotiating with Israel's leaders. They requested that Israel avoid striking back against Iraq. Israel, a Jewish nation, had a long history of hostilities with other Middle Eastern countries. U.S. leaders feared that those other Middle Eastern countries might take Saddam's side if Israel fought back. Their dislike of Israel could potentially outweigh their desire to remove Saddam from Kuwait.

Israel announced on January 20 that it would not wage war against Iraq. The United States provided Israel with air-defense missiles to help the small nation defend itself against further attacks. Iraq continued attacking Israel throughout the war. But the country honored its commitment to the coalition.

Retreating Iraqi military forces set fire to 700 oil wells, which burned from January and February 1991 to November 1991.

Dirty Fighting

On the same day Israel announced that it would not retaliate, Iraqi television broadcasts showed several captured UN airmen. They appeared to have been beaten and tortured. International laws state that prisoners of war are not to be physically or mentally tortured. Saddam made it even clearer that he was unwilling to play by the rules of war when he showed these men on television. President Bush vowed that Saddam would pay for this cruel treatment of UN captives.

Iraqi troops began a campaign of destroying Kuwait's natural resources. Beginning on January 21, they blew up Kuwait's oil wells, destroying important resources and causing massive environmental damage. They began pouring oil into the Persian Gulf four days later. Millions of gallons of thick oil spread quickly and poisoned wildlife. The spill was 31 miles (50 km) long and reached 8 miles (13 km) out from the coast after just one day. The spill became so large that it began to threaten the Saudi water supply. As a desert country, Saudi Arabia drew saltwater from the gulf and used **desalination** plants to make it drinkable.

General Colin Powell

Colin Powell was born on April 5, 1937, in New York City. He joined the U.S. Army after graduating from college and served in the Vietnam War in the 1960s. In 1989, Powell was promoted to the rank of four-star general. That year, he became the first African American to serve as chairman of the Joint Chiefs of Staff. In this position, he helped plan and organize military operations in the Persian Gulf War with General Schwarzkopf. Powell entered politics in the late 1990s. In 2001, he became the first African American secretary of state.

A ground assault was necessary to force Iraq out of Kuwait.

Planning for a Ground Assault

Dick Cheney and Colin Powell met with General Schwarzkopf in Saudi Arabia on February 9 to begin planning for a possible ground assault. The only fighting that had occurred on the ground so far had been minor incidents along the Saudi border. It would soon be necessary to fight on land if Saddam continued to hold Kuwait.

The Iranian foreign minister announced ten days later that discussions with Iraqi officials had indicated that Iraq was willing to withdraw without special terms. A Soviet spokesman made a similar announcement soon afterward. But this version of the story included conditions that Iraq had requested. First, Iraq would not withdraw unless trade bans were lifted once two-thirds of their troops had left Kuwait. Second, they demanded that all UN resolutions against them be lifted. This would free the country from having to pay Kuwait for the damage its forces had done.

Saddam made a radio speech on the same day the Soviet spokesman announced this plan. He spoke out against Arab nations in the Middle East who refused to support Iraq. He called them traitors for siding with the Western nations. He made no mention of any peace plan during the speech.

On February 22, Iraq requested six weeks to begin removing troops from Kuwait. The UN forces immediately rejected this request. They demanded that Iraq begin withdrawing by 5:00 p.m. on February 23. They also demanded that the withdrawal be complete within a week. The coalition threatened a ground war if Saddam failed to observe these conditions.

Operation Desert Sabre

Saddam once again ignored all warnings from the UN forces. The Iraqi forces remained in place as the deadline for withdrawal passed on the evening of February 23. The UN ground forces launched Operation Desert Sabre just a few hours later, in the early morning of February 24.

General Schwarzkopf believed that the Iraqis would expect an attack by sea along the Persian Gulf coast. So he concentrated the UN forces on the western border of Kuwait. The numerous and powerful UN troops made their way into Kuwait. Thousands of Iraqi troops gave up without a fight. About 5,500 Iraqi soldiers were captured in the first day. There were very few losses for the UN coalition.

The UN forces surrounded Kuwait City on February 25. More than 20,000 Iraqis were captured. That number increased to 63,000 by the next day. Kuwaiti resistance fighters joined in the battle. They helped to free the U.S. Embassy in Kuwait City from Iraqi soldiers. UN aircraft dropped bombs that killed about 10,000 Iraqi soldiers attempting to leave along the highways connecting Kuwait and Iraq.

Saddam gave a radio speech in which he claimed that Iraq was not giving up but simply withdrawing because of "current circumstances." He claimed that Kuwait would remain a part of Iraq even after the withdrawal.

Thousands of UN soldiers surrounded Kuwait City on February 25, 1991.

Victorious Kuwaitis celebrated in the streets of Kuwait City when the war ended.

Victory

The UN Security Council met in New York City once again on February 26. They discussed the details of ending the war. A representative from Iraq confirmed that the Iraqi forces were in the process of withdrawing. He asked for a cease-fire so they could leave peacefully. The council rejected this request. It stated that the war would continue until all Iraqi troops were forcefully ejected from Kuwait. Only those who were unarmed would be spared.

Kuwait's flag was raised in Kuwait City the next day. The UN coalition ground forces had achieved victory in only 100 hours. Just 134 U.S. military members were killed. Tens of thousands of Iraqis had been killed or wounded. It was as clear as a victory could be.

CHAPTER 4

AFTERMATH

Iraqi soldiers held up white flags to indicate their surrender.

At a UN Security Council session on February 27, Iraq agreed to follow all requests made by UN forces and to release all captives. In return, the UN forces began a conditional cease-fire on February 28. The coalition promised not to attack withdrawing Iraqi forces as long as they left peacefully and did not fire missiles on Israel.

A FIRSTHAND LOOK AT THE UNITED NATIONS

The United Nations Headquarters is located in New York City, New York. Representatives from countries around the world meet there to discuss international issues such as wars and trade agreements. You can visit the headquarters and take tours of the rooms where UN representatives made decisions about the Persian Gulf War. See page 60 for a link to learn more about the United Nations.

Wrapping Up the War

Even with the cease-fire in effect, the Iraqis found ways to cause trouble. Part of the cease-fire terms banned the Iraqis from flying planes. This was done to prevent them from launching surprise attacks. Because many of the bridges between Kuwait and Iraq had been destroyed,

Even after the war had ended, some Iraqi soldiers continued to resist UN peacekeeping forces.

Kuwait's night sky is lit by raging oil well fires in the distance.

Iraqi military leaders requested that they be allowed to fly helicopters. General Schwarzkopf granted their request.

The Iraqis were not entirely honest about their intentions. They used the helicopters to drop bombs on rebellious Shiites in southern Iraq instead of flying troops back to Iraq. Many of the Shiites tried to flee the country. They were stopped at the border by UN forces. These forces were unaware of the bombings.

Saddam did everything he could to convince the people of Iraq that the war had not resulted in defeat.

Saddam Hussein refused to admit defeat.

On February 28, he gave a radio speech claiming that his goal had simply been to teach the Western world a lesson. He stated that Iraq had been successful in accomplishing this goal.

Rebuilding Kuwait

About one-third of Kuwait's land had been destroyed by the end of the war. Iraqi soldiers had set fire to more than 700 Kuwaiti oil wells. This was a huge waste of valuable oil and harmful to the environment. Thick clouds of smoke carried oil droplets all around the surrounding land. This oil began to form a thick coating of tar over the soil as it fell to the ground and dried. In some places, the tar layers were as thick as 5 inches (12.7 centimeters). The oil formed large pools in other areas. Chemicals from the oil seeped down into the soil. They poisoned the local water supplies.

SPOTLIGHT ON

Oil Well Fires

By September 1991, 27 international firefighting teams had arrived in Kuwait to help put out the oil well fires. The first fires were put out using water from the nearby Persian Gulf. Firefighters pumped up to 4,000 gallons (15,140 liters) per minute through pipelines that had previously been used to transport oil.

Another method was to build tall cases around the fires. This raised the flames above the wells. Firefighters then pumped water or chemicals into the case. The fire's oxygen supply was cut off. In other instances, they drilled new wells into the sides of the burning wells. This cut off the flow of oil to the fires. Firefighters had extinguished hundreds of fires by November 1991.

Firefighters shield themselves with metal barriers while battling the oil well fires.

Thousands of environmental experts from around the world came together to help the people of Kuwait clean the countryside and put out oil fires. Their hard work helped clean up the mess in less than nine months.

Iraqi troops had buried underground land mines in parts of the country during their time in Kuwait. Someone could easily walk over one and not know it, until it exploded. Some areas remained dangerous for years afterward. As a result many Kuwaitis were injured long after the war was over.

Even the normal events of war had damaged the environment. The Iraqis had crushed the top layers of Kuwait's soil by digging trenches and driving heavy tanks throughout many parts of the country. The soil was ground into a fine powder that easily blew away. Buildings and farms were covered in thick layers of dust. The fighting had

Tensions remain high between Kuwait and Iraq even today. On January 10, 2011, gunfire broke out in the Persian Gulf between an Iraqi fishing boat and a Kuwaiti Coast Guard boat. This was not the first time Iraqi fishing boats had entered into violent conflicts with Kuwaiti vessels. The Kuwaiti government claimed that the Iraqi boat had violated boundaries and entered Kuwaiti waters. They also claimed that the Iraqi fishermen were smugglers. Iraqi leaders claimed that the fishermen were unarmed and had not entered Kuwaiti waters.

destroyed many buildings and roads. It would take many years before Kuwait fully recovered from the destruction.

Dealing with Saddam

Though the war had ended, the United Nations knew that Saddam was still a threat. He possessed a great deal of powerful weaponry. It was only a matter of time before he struck again. The United Nations passed Resolution 687 in April 1991. It required Saddam to make a list of Iraq's nuclear, chemical, and biological weapons. Countries could better decide how to deal with Saddam if they knew what they were up against.

UN officials later destroyed biological weapon ingredients found in Iraq.

Fermentation vats such as these could possibly have been used by Iraq to manufacture biological weapons.

According to the resolution, there would be a worldwide ban on Iraqi oil exports until the list was delivered.

Even with such threats, Saddam attempted to hide his weapons from UN inspectors. UN forces were attacked when they arrived to search Iraq's weapons storage bunkers. Nonetheless, inspectors were able to secure documents showing that Iraq had a highly developed nuclear weapons program. Though Saddam had been defeated in Kuwait, he would surely continue to be an enemy in the future.

MAP OF THE EVENTS

What Happened Where?

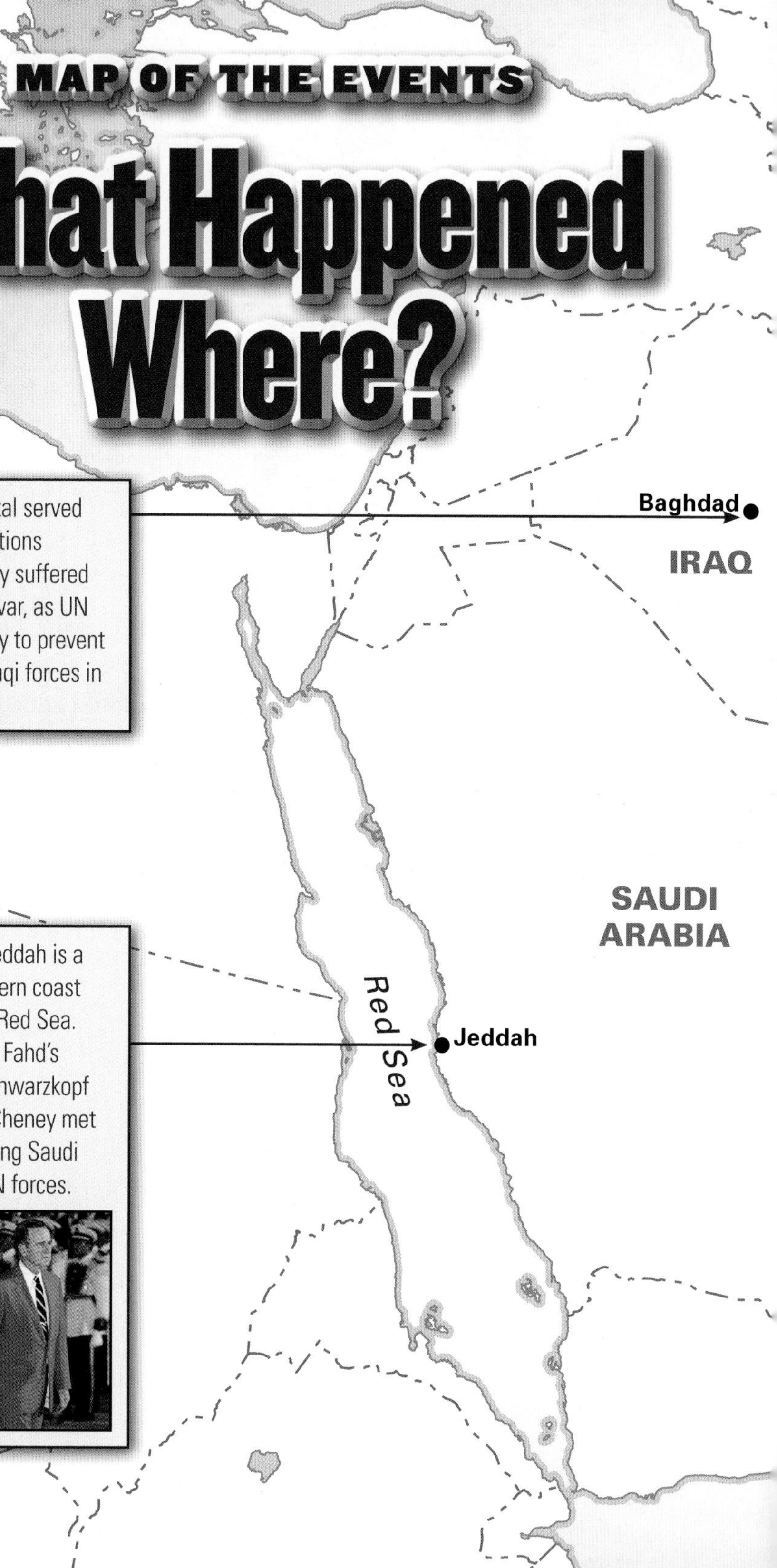

Baghdad, Iraq Iraq's capital served as Saddam's base of operations throughout the war. The city suffered heavy damage during the war, as UN forces bombed it repeatedly to prevent communication with the Iraqi forces in Kuwait.

Jeddah, Saudi Arabia Jeddah is a major port city on the western coast of Saudi Arabia, along the Red Sea. It was home to one of King Fahd's palaces, where General Schwarzkopf and Secretary of Defense Cheney met with the king to discuss using Saudi Arabia as a base for the UN forces.

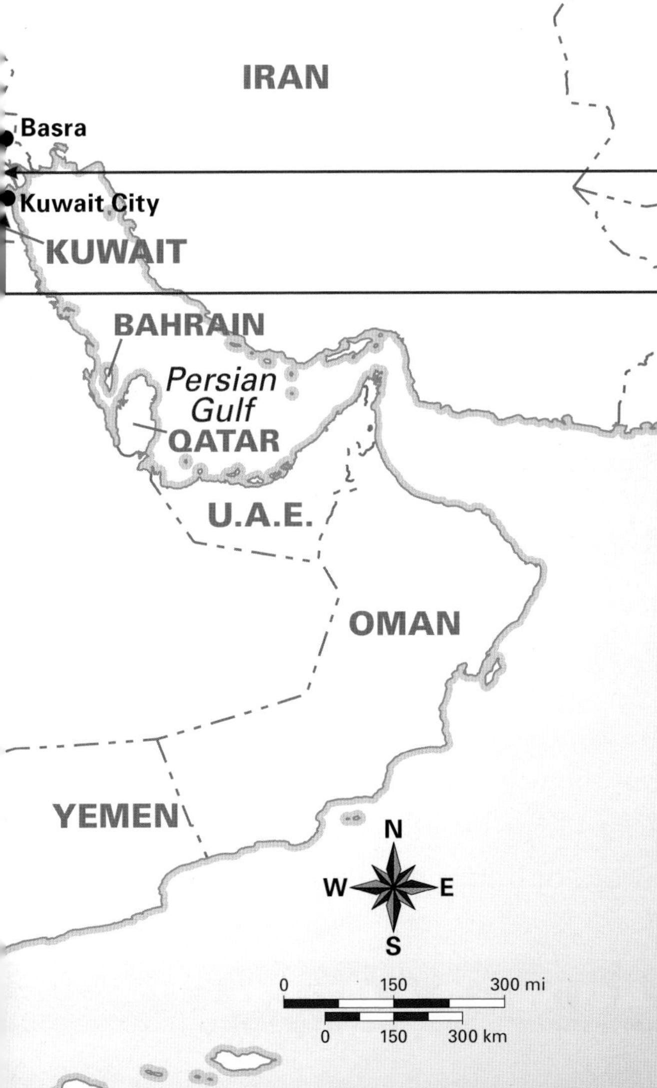

Highway 80, leading from Kuwait City to Basra, Iraq More than 10,000 Iraqi soldiers were killed as they tried to escape Kuwait using this highway at the end of the war. Many of their vehicles were filled with stolen Kuwaiti goods that they had quickly grabbed as they fled. As traffic backed up, UN aircraft bombed the highway, preventing Iraqi forces from escaping.

Kuwait City, Kuwait Kuwait's capital city is home to Kuwaiti leaders and a large population. It was an obvious first choice of targets for the Iraqi military when they began their invasion.

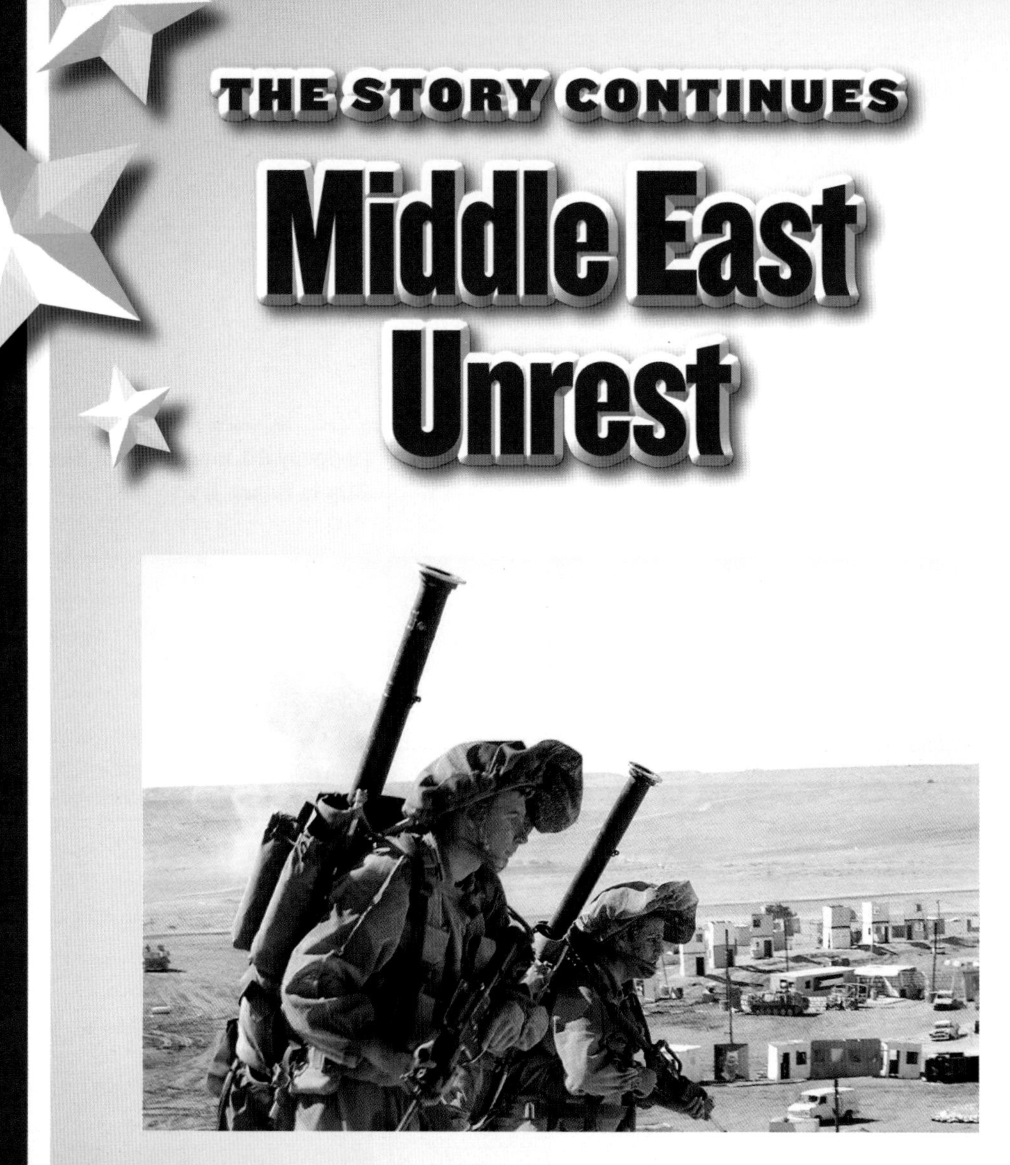

THE STORY CONTINUES

Middle East Unrest

The Iraq War grew out of the conflict that began during the Gulf War.

Trade restrictions against Iraq were enforced heavily in the years following the war. Tension continued to build. In 2003, U.S. and British forces began to gather once again at the border of Iraq. This time, they did not wait for approval from the United Nations. U.S. president George W. Bush, son of President George H. W. Bush, demanded that Saddam step down. When Saddam refused, the Iraq War began on March 20, 2003.

Saddam was captured by U.S. forces on December 13, 2003. He was turned over to Iraqi authorities. In 2005, he was put on trial by the new Iraqi leadership. He was executed the following year.

Even with Saddam out of the picture, the Middle East continues to be one of the most unstable regions in the world. In early 2011, several countries experienced significant rebellions by citizens who were unhappy with their countries' leadership. Only time will tell what the future holds for the people of Iraq, Kuwait, and the rest of the Middle East.

Saddam Hussein at his trial in 2005.

ON AUGUST 31, 2010.

King Fahd (1921–2005) was the Saudi ruler who allowed UN forces to enter his country and conduct the war from within its borders.

George H. W. Bush (1924–) was the 41st president of the United States, serving his term during the Persian Gulf War. He was vice president from 1981 to 1989 under President Ronald Reagan.

Sheikh Jaber (1926–2006) was the Kuwaiti leader who was driven from his country when Iraq invaded.

Norman Schwarzkopf (1934–) was commander in chief of the U.S. Central Command and led all UN coalition forces during the war.

Norman Schwarzkopf

Saddam Hussein (1937–2006) was the president of Iraq and a leading member of the Ba'ath Party, who ordered the invasion of Kuwait.

Colin Powell (1937–) was a U.S. general who served as chairman of the Joint Chiefs of Staff during the war.

Dick Cheney (1941–) was the U.S. secretary of defense during the war and later served as vice president from 2001 to 2009 under President George W. Bush.

Saddam Hussein

TIMELINE

1979

July 16
Saddam Hussein takes control of Iraq.

1980–1988

Iraq builds its military as it fights in the Iran-Iraq War.

1990

July
Iraqi forces gather along the border with Kuwait.

August 2
Iraq invades Kuwait.

August 8
UN coalition forces move into Saudi Arabia.

December 18
United Nations declares that Iraq must withdraw from Kuwait by January 15, 1991, or be attacked.

1991

January 12
U.S. Congress votes to wage war against Iraq.

January 16
Persian Gulf War begins.

January 18
Iraq begins firing missiles at Israel.

January 21
Iraq begins blowing up Kuwaiti oil wells.

January 25
Iraq begins dumping oil into the Persian Gulf.

February 24
UN ground campaign begins.

February 27
War ends as Iraqi troops are driven from Kuwait City.

Primary sources provide firsthand evidence about a topic. Witnesses to a historical event create primary sources. They include autobiographies, newspaper reports of the time, oral histories, photographs, and memoirs. A secondary source analyzes primary sources, and is one step or more removed from the event. Secondary sources include textbooks, encyclopedias, and commentaries.

April Glaspie Report After meeting with Saddam Hussein in July 1990, April Glaspie filed a report with U.S. government officials outlining her conversation with the leader of Iraq. Her report can be read in its entirety at *www.washingtonpost.com/wp-srv/politics/documents/glaspie1-13.pdf?sid=ST2008040203634*

Bush's "This Will Not Stand" News Conference, August 5, 1990 Following Iraq's invasion of Kuwait, President George H. W. Bush met with members of the press and delivered his strong reaction to Saddam Hussein's act of aggression. A *New York Times* report of his news conference can be found at *www.nytimes.com/1990/08/06/world/iraqi-invasion-bush-hinting-force-declares-iraqi-assault-will-not-stand-proxy.html?scp=1&sq=august+6%2C+1990+this+will+not+stand&st=nyt*

President Bush's Speech Announcing the Start of the Persian Gulf War, January 16, 1991 An audio recording of the president's address to the American people explaining the causes of the war can be found at *www.history.com/topics/persian-gulf-war/audio#george-hw-bush-announces-start-of-persian-gulf-war*

United Nations Visitors Centre Located in New York City, the United Nations offers guided tours of the General Assembly Hall, a variety of exhibits, and firsthand audio recordings that bring to life historical UN moments. For more information, visit *http://visit.un.org/wcm/content/*

Books

Augustin, Byron, and Jake Kubena. *Iraq*. New York: Children's Press, 2006.

Crawford, Steve. *The First Gulf War*. Reading, CT: Brown Bear Books, 2009.

Friedman, Mel. *Iraq*. New York: Children's Press, 2009.

Perritano, John. *Desert Storm*. New York: Franklin Watts, 2010.

Rice, Earle. *Overview of the Persian Gulf War, 1990*. Hockessin, DE: Mitchell Lane Publishers, 2009.

Willis, Terri. *Kuwait*. New York: Children's Press, 2007.

Web Sites

History.com—Persian Gulf War

www.history.com/topics/persian-gulf-war

Listen to President Bush's speech announcing the start of the war and read about some of the war's most important people.

PBS Frontline: The Gulf War

www.pbs.org/wgbh/pages/frontline/gulf/

Watch videos, check out maps, and listen to war stories directly from the soldiers who fought in Kuwait.

GLOSSARY

artillery (ar-TIL-uh-ree) large weapons that are fired from a distance, such as missile launchers

coalition (koh-uh-LISH-uhn) a group of allied forces

desalination (dee-say-lih-NAY-shuhn) a process that removes salt from water

divisions (di-VIZH-uhnz) large military units

inflation (in-FLAY-shuhn) a general increase in prices, causing money to be worth less

nerve gas (NERV GAS) poisonous gas that affects the nervous system

petroleum (puh-TROH-lee-uhm) a thick, oily liquid used to make gasoline and oil

quota (KWOH-tuh) a fixed amount of something

rations (RASH-uhnz) small amounts of something shared among a group

resistance (ri-ZISS-tuhnss) fighting back

retaliation (ri-tal-ee-AY-shuhn) action taken in response to an attack

United Nations (yoo-NITE-ed NAY-shuhns) an international organization designed to promote peace and cooperation between countries

weapons of mass destruction (WEP-uhnz UHV MASS di-STRUHK-shuhn) weapons designed to kill large numbers of civilians and military units

Page numbers in *italics* indicate illustrations.

Josh Gregory received a BA in English at the University of Missouri-Columbia. He lives in Chicago, Illinois.